VICTOR R. FUCHS

THE GROWING IMPORTANCE OF THE SERVICE INDUSTRIES

OCCASIONAL PAPER 96

NATIONAL BUREAU OF ECONOMIC RESEARCH

NEW YORK 1965

Distributed by COLUMBIA UNIVERSITY PRESS

NEW YORK AND LONDON

H 11
.N2382
no. 96
Law

Library of Congress Catalog Card Number 65-29209
National Bureau of Economic Research, Inc.
261 Madison Avenue, New York, N.Y. 10016

Gift of
Prof. Landes

This is a study by the National Bureau of Economic Research. It is reprinted, with minor changes, from the October 1965 issue of *The Journal of Business*

NATIONAL BUREAU OF ECONOMIC RESEARCH
1965

OFFICERS

Frank W. Fetter, *Chairman*
Arthur F. Burns, *President*
Theodore O. Yntema, *Vice-President*
Donald B. Woodward, *Treasurer*
William J. Carson, *Secretary*

Geoffrey H. Moore, *Director of Research*
Douglas H. Eldridge, *Executive Director*
Hal B. Lary, *Associate Director of Research*
Victor R. Fuchs, *Associate Director of Research*

DIRECTORS AT LARGE

Robert B. Anderson, *New York City*
Wallace J. Campbell, *Foundation for Cooperative Housing*
Erwin D. Canham, *Christian Science Monitor*
Solomon Fabricant, *New York University*
Marion B. Folsom, *Eastman Kodak Company*
Crawford H. Greenewalt, *E. I. du Pont de Nemours & Company*
Gabriel Hauge, *Manufacturers Hanover Trust Company*
A. J. Hayes, *International Association of Machinists*
Walter W. Heller, *University of Minnesota*
Albert J. Hettinger, Jr., *Lazard Frères and Company*

H. W. Laidler, *League for Industrial Democracy*
Geoffrey H. Moore, *National Bureau of Economic Research*
Charles G. Mortimer, *General Foods Corporation*
J. Wilson Newman, *Dun & Bradstreet, Inc.*
George B. Roberts, *Larchmont, New York*
Harry Scherman, *Book-of-the-Month Club*
Boris Shishkin, *American Federation of Labor and Congress of Industrial Organizations*
George Soule, *South Kent, Connecticut*
Gus Tyler, *International Ladies' Garment Workers' Union*
Joseph H. Willits, *Langhorne, Pennsylvania*

Donald B. Woodward, *A. W. Jones and Company*

DIRECTORS BY UNIVERSITY APPOINTMENT

V. W. Bladen, *Toronto*
Francis M. Boddy, *Minnesota*
Arthur F. Burns, *Columbia*
Lester V. Chandler, *Princeton*
Melvin G. de Chazeau, *Cornell*
Frank W. Fetter, *Northwestern*
R. A. Gordon, *California*

Harold M. Groves, *Wisconsin*
Gottfried Haberler, *Harvard*
Maurice W. Lee, *North Carolina*
Lloyd G. Reynolds, *Yale*
Paul A. Samuelson, *Massachusetts Institute of Technology*
Theodore W. Schultz, *Chicago*

Willis J. Winn, *Pennsylvania*

DIRECTORS BY APPOINTMENT OF OTHER ORGANIZATIONS

Percival F. Brundage, *American Institute of Certified Public Accountants*
Nathaniel Goldfinger, *American Federation of Labor and Congress of Industrial Organizations*
Harold G. Halcrow, *American Farm Economic Association*
Murray Shields, *American Management Association*

Willard L. Thorp, *American Economic Association*
W. Allen Wallis, *American Statistical Association*
Harold F. Williamson, *Economic History Association*
Theodore O. Yntema, *Committee for Economic Development*

DIRECTORS EMERITI

Shepard Morgan, *Norfolk, Connecticut*
N. I. Stone, *New York City*
Jacob Viner, *Princeton, New Jersey*

RESEARCH STAFF

Moses Abramovitz
Gary S. Becker
William H. Brown, Jr.
Gerhard Bry
Arthur F. Burns
Phillip Cagan
Frank G. Dickinson
James S. Earley
Richard A. Easterlin
Solomon Fabricant

Albert Fishlow
Milton Friedman
Victor R. Fuchs
H. G. Georgiadis
Raymond W. Goldsmith
Jack M. Guttentag
Challis A. Hall, Jr.
Daniel M. Holland
Thor Hultgren
F. Thomas Juster

C. Harry Kahn
John W. Kendrick
Irving B. Kravis
Hal B. Lary
Robert E. Lipsey
Ruth P. Mack
Jacob Mincer
Ilse Mintz
Geoffrey H. Moore
Roger F. Murray

Ralph L. Nelson
G. Warren Nutter
Richard T. Selden
Lawrence H. Seltzer
Robert P. Shay
George J. Stigler
Norman B. Ture
Herbert B. Woolley
Victor Zarnowitz

RELATION OF THE DIRECTORS TO THE WORK AND PUBLICATIONS OF THE NATIONAL BUREAU OF ECONOMIC RESEARCH

1. The object of the National Bureau of Economic Research is to ascertain and to present to the public important economic facts and their interpretation in a scientific and impartial manner. The Board of Directors is charged with the responsibility of ensuring that the work of the National Bureau is carried on in strict conformity with this object.

2. To this end the Board of Directors shall appoint one or more Directors of Research.

3. The Director or Directors of Research shall submit to the members of the Board, or to its Executive Committee, for their formal adoption, all specific proposals concerning researches to be instituted.

4. No report shall be published until the Director or Directors of Research shall have submitted to the Board a summary drawing attention to the character of the data and their utilization in the report, the nature and treatment of the problems involved, the main conclusions, and such other information as in their opinion would serve to determine the suitability of the report for publication in accordance with the principles of the National Bureau.

5. A copy of any manuscript proposed for publication shall also be submitted to each member of the Board. For each manuscript to be so submitted a special committee shall be appointed by the President, or at his designation by the Executive Director, consisting of three Directors selected as nearly as may be one from each general division of the Board. The names of the special manuscript committee shall be stated to each Director when the summary and report described in paragraph (4) are sent to him. It shall be the duty of each member of the committee to read the manuscript. If each member of the special committee signifies his approval within thirty days, the manuscript may be published. If each member of the special committee has not signified his approval within thirty days of the transmittal of the report and manuscript, the Director of Research shall then notify each member of the Board, requesting approval or disapproval of publication, and thirty additional days shall be granted for this purpose. The manuscript shall then not be published unless at least a majority of the entire Board and a two-thirds majority of those members of the Board who shall have voted on the proposal within the time fixed for the receipt of votes on the publication proposed shall have approved.

6. No manuscript may be published, though approved by each member of the special committee, until forty-five days have elapsed from the transmittal of the summary and report. The interval is allowed for the receipt of any memorandum of dissent or reservation, together with a brief statement of his reasons, that any member may wish to express; and such memorandum of dissent or reservation shall be published with the manuscript if he so desires. Publication does not, however, imply that each member of the Board has read the manuscript, or that either members of the Board in general, or of the special committee, have passed upon its validity in every detail.

7. A copy of this resolution shall, unless otherwise determined by the Board, be printed in each copy of every National Bureau book.

(Resolution adopted October 25, 1926, as revised February 6, 1933, and February 24, 1941)

THE GROWING IMPORTANCE OF THE SERVICE INDUSTRIES*

VICTOR R. FUCHS

> The economics of tertiary industry remains to be written. Many as yet feel uncomfortable about even admitting their existence.
>
> COLIN CLARK, *The Conditions of Economic Progress*

INTRODUCTION

THIS paper begins with the observation that virtually all of the net growth of employment in the United States in the postwar period has occurred in the service sector. As a result, this sector (comprising trade, finance, insurance, and real estate; personal, professional, business, and repair services; and general government) now accounts for more than half of total employment and more than half of gross national product. This country is pioneering in a new stage of economic development. We are now a "service economy"—that is, we are the first nation in the history of the world in which more than half of the employed population is not involved in the production of food, clothing, houses, automobiles, and other tangible goods.[1]

Although the shift of employment to the service industries has been particularly dramatic in the postwar period, it was also in evidence prior to the war, as may be seen in Table 1 and Figures 1 and 2. The table shows employment by sector for selected years since 1929. Some industrial detail is also presented in explicit recognition of the partly arbitrary character of the sector definitions. These definitions arise in part from our interest in a group of industries that have not received much attention in the past from economists concerned with productivity analysis. The boundary between service and goods production is very difficult to draw, and probably no division based on industrial classifications would be completely satisfactory. One could refer to the industries studied in this paper simply as "group 1" and "group 2"; but for convenience, and because it generally conforms to convention, they are designated as the service and goods sectors.

In addition to the full sector comparisons, data are presented for modified sectors denoted by asterisks. Goods* is the

---

* This paper is the second to appear as part of the National Bureau's study of productivity in the service industries, undertaken with the assistance of a grant from the Ford Foundation. A grant of electronic computer time by the International Business Machines Corporation was used for some of the statistical analyses in this report.

I have benefited from comments by Gary S. Becker, Daniel Creamer, Solomon Fabricant, Robert E. Lipsey, Jacob Mincer, Geoffrey H. Moore, and David Schwartzman. The reading committee of the National Bureau's board of directors—Walter W. Heller, Maurice W. Lee, and Donald B. Woodward—made many helpful suggestions. I am pleased to acknowledge the research assistance of Judy Mitnick, Linda Nasif, Regina Reibstein, Katherine Warden, and especially Irving Leveson. I am also grateful to James F. McRee, Jr., who prepared the manuscript for press; to H. Irving Forman, who drew the figures; and to Joyce M. Rose, for secretarial and editorial assistance.

[1] One dramatic example of this shift is that the *increase* in employment in education between 1950 and 1960 was greater than the *total* employment in primary metal industries in either year.

TABLE 1
Persons Engaged by Sector and Major Industry Group, Selected Years, 1929–63
(Thousands)

	1929	1937	1948	1953	1957	1963
Goods[a]	27,561	25,989	31,764	33,286	32,767	31,445
Service[a]	18,655	21,167	26,812	31,779	33,807	37,962
Goods*[b]	17,947	16,651	24,032	26,559	26,433	25,733
Service*[b]	12,263	12,596	17,107	18,767	20,323	22,547
Agriculture, forestry, and fishing	9,205	8,864	7,012	5,885	5,470	4,725
Mining	1,017	993	1,021	896	858	654
Construction	2,306	1,738	3,262	3,801	4,161	4,305
Manufacturing	10,556	10,686	15,468	17,462	17,054	16,767
Transportation	3,034	2,333	3,000	2,997	2,846	2,546
Communications and public utilities	1,034	901	1,281	1,403	1,514	1,461
Government enterprise	409	474	720	842	864	987
Wholesale trade	1,744	1,857	2,712	2,971	3,205	3,391
Retail trade	6,077	6,305	8,597	9,311	9,775	10,537
Finance and insurance	1,207	1,065	1,349	1,705	2,040	2,437
Real estate	368	455	574	615	681	763
Households and institutions	3,249	3,060	3,051	3,246	3,749	4,316
Professional, personal, business, and repair services	3,235	3,369	4,449	4,780	5,303	6,182
General government (including armed forces)	2,775	5,056	6,080	9,151	9,054	10,336

[a] Goods = agriculture, mining, construction, manufacturing, transportation, communications and public utilities, and government enterprise; service = wholesale and retail trade, finance and insurance, real estate, services, and general government.
[b] Goods* = goods excluding agriculture and government enterprise; service* = service excluding real estate, households and institutions, and general government.
Source: Office of Business Economics; *Survey of Current Business*, July, 1964; *U.S. Income and Output*, 1958; *National Income, 1954 Edition*.

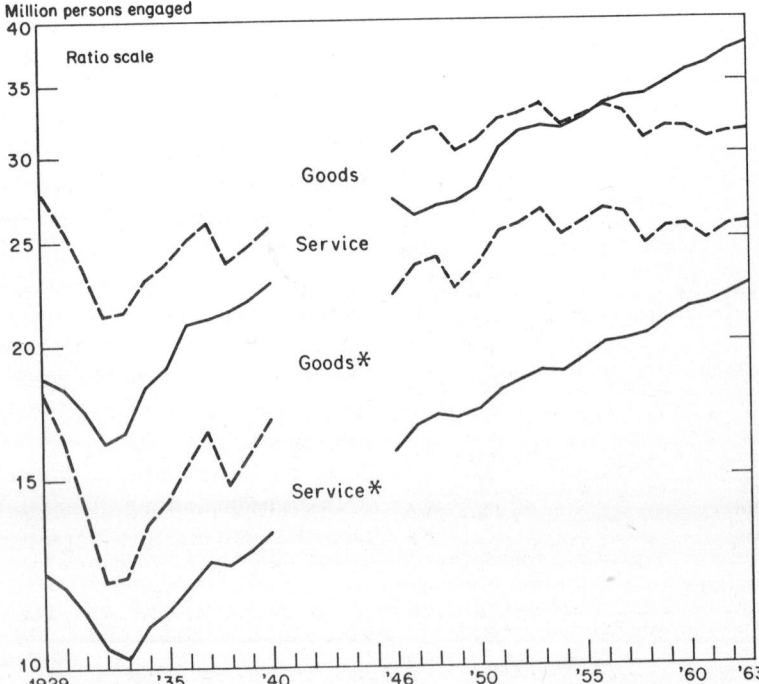

Fig. 1.—Persons engaged by sector, 1929–40, 1946–63. See Table 1 for sector definitions. Source: U.S. Department of Commerce, Office of Business Economics.

goods sector minus agriculture and government enterprises. Service* is the service sector minus real estate, households and institutions, and government.[2] Other sector definitions could be introduced as well, but the basic point concerning the growing relative importance of services would be unaffected by any reasonable changes in definition.

Figures 1 and 2 show sector employment in absolute terms and as a percentage of total employment annually, 1929 through 1963. The war years are omitted

[2] The excluded industries present special problems in the measurement of inputs and outputs.

because the changes in employment patterns caused by the war are largely irrelevant for the study of long-term trends. Some differences between the prewar and postwar trends may be noted. The full service sector increased its share of employment in both periods, but the relative growth of the modified service sector occurred almost entirely after the war. Similarly, while the share of the full goods sector has been decreasing steadily, the modified goods sector was above its 1929 level in the decade 1946–56. It is only in recent years that the other goods industries have joined agriculture

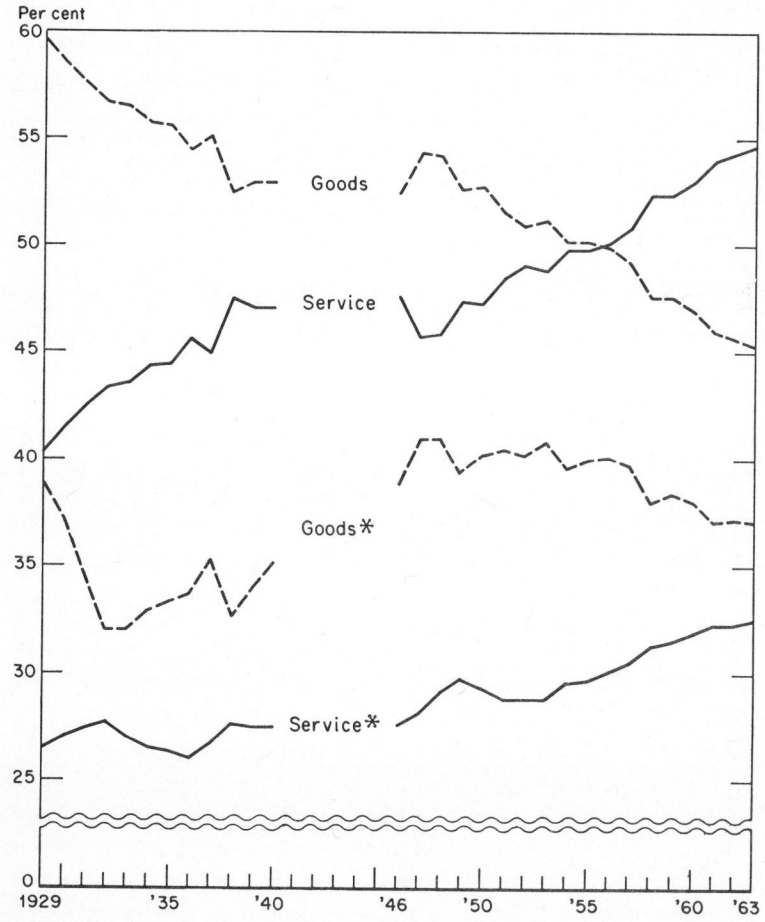

FIG. 2.—Sector employment as percentage of total employment, 1929–40, 1946–63. Source: see Fig. 1

as a declining fraction of total employment.

In this paper I propose to explore three questions concerning the relative growth of the service sector: (1) Why did the shift occur? (2) What are the implications for the economy? (3) What are the implications for economic analysis? The answers that will be suggested are not based on completed, tested research. They are rather akin to working hypotheses. Some of them are currently being explored in the National Bureau's study of productivity in the service industries.[3]

A MORE DETAILED LOOK AT THE GROWTH OF SERVICES

Before considering possible explanations for the increase in the service sector's share of total employment, several aspects of this increase should be explored. First, let us see whether the differential growth has been true for individual industries as well as for the sector aggregate. Table 2 provides an affirmative answer to this question.

Average annual rates of change of employment (1929–63) by industry have been calculated at the sixty-one–industry level of detail provided by the National Income Division of the Office of Business Economics. Thirty-eight of the industries are in the goods sector; twenty-three in the service sector. The fraction of the industries in each sector experiencing different annual rates of growth is also shown.

We see that a large percentage of the service industries had rapid rates of growth of employment and only a very few had negative or slow rates. For the goods industries, the reverse is true. Almost one-third of the goods industries showed an absolute decline in employment between 1929 and 1963, while fewer than one-sixth of them had rates of growth in excess of 2.5 per cent per annum. Only two of the service industries showed declines in employment and almost half of them grew at rates exceeding 2.5 per cent. The median rates of growth were 2.14 for the service industries, 0.99 for the goods, and 1.43 for all industries.

If the sixty-one industries are grouped by sector, and by whether they grew faster or slower than 1.43 per cent per annum, the difference between sectors is statistically significant at the 95 per cent level of confidence, according to the χ^2 test. It appears that the generalization about the shift of employment to services has considerable validity at the detailed industry level, as well as for the sector aggregate.

A second question concerns the extent to which a classification of employment by function instead of industry would confirm the existence of a trend toward services. We do not have employment data by function, but we do have information concerning the occupational distribution of the labor force, and the latter more closely approaches function than do the data for industries.

In Table 3, the eleven major occupation groups have been classified as "service type" or "goods type" according to their industrial distribution in 1960. We see that the former group has grown rapidly (2.1 per cent per annum between 1930 and 1960), while the "goods-type" occupations showed no net change over the period. Moderate gains in some goods-producing occupations were offset by absolute declines in others. Thus the

[3] Some preliminary findings of this study are reported in Victor R. Fuchs, *Productivity Trends in the Goods and Service Sectors, 1929–61: A Preliminary Survey* (Occasional Paper 89). (New York: National Bureau of Economic Research, 1964.) Other work now in progress at the National Bureau includes studies of wholesale and retail trade, state and local government, personal services, health, and changes in the quality of labor.

TABLE 2
RATE OF GROWTH OF EMPLOYMENT,[a] GOODS AND SERVICE INDUSTRIES, 1929–63

Average Annual Rate of Change of Employment (Per Cent)	All Industries in Sector (Per Cent)	Goods Industries	All Industries in Sector (Per Cent)	Service Industries
2.5 and over	15.8	Electric machinery[b] Transportation equipment except auto Air transportation (common carrier) Highway freight transportation and warehousing Radio and TV broadcast State and local government enterprise	43.5	Finance, n.e.c. Insurance carriers Commercial and trade schools and employment agencies Business services, n.e.c. Miscellaneous repair services and hand trades Medical and other health services Engineering and other professional services Educational services, n.e.c. Nonprofit membership organizations, n.e.c. Federal general government State and local general government
1.5–2.49	21.0	Crude petroleum natural gas Contract construction Chemical and allied products[b] Rubber products Metal products, etc.[b] Paper and allied products Federal government enterprise Machinery except electric[b]	26.0	Wholesale trade Retail trade Banking Insurance agents and combination offers Real estate Legal services
0–1.49	31.6	Agriculture services, forests and fishing Non-metal mining and quarrying Food and kindred products Apparel and other finished products Printing, publishing, etc. Petroleum and coal products[b] Stone, clay, and glass products Auto and auto equipment Services allied to transportation Telephone, telegraph, etc. Utilities, electricity, and gas Local utilities and public service, n.e.c.	21.7	Hotels and other lodging Personal services Motion pictures Amusement and recreation except motion pictures
Negative	31.6	Farms Metal mining Anthracite mining Bituminous and other soft coal mining Tobacco manufacturing Textile mill products Lumber and furniture[b] Leather products Railroads Local and highway passenger transportation Water transportation Pipeline transportation	8.7	Security and commodity brokers Private households

[a] Employment is measured "by persons engaged," which includes wage and salary workers reduced to full-time equivalents plus self-employed. Unpaid family workers are not included.
[b] Industry definition not strictly comparable throughout period.
Source: 1929, *National Income, 1954 Edition*, Table 28, pp. 202–3; 1963, *Survey of Current Business*, July, 1964, Table 55, p. 30.

occupational data suggest that the industry shift in employment, far from exaggerating the shift in function, may actually understate it.

We are primarily concerned with comparing goods-producing and service-producing industries, but it should be noted that in the national income accounts a distinction between goods and services is made on the basis of final expenditure.

fication also shows a more rapid rate of growth for services in current and constant dollars.

The final point to be made in this section is that the shift of employment to services does not represent a sudden departure from previous long-term trends. For as long as we have records on the industrial distribution of the labor force, we find a secular tendency for the per-

TABLE 3

OCCUPATIONAL DISTRIBUTION OF LABOR FORCE, 1930 AND 1960

	PER CENT OF OCCUPATION EMPLOYED IN SERVICE SECTOR, 1960	LABOR FORCE (MILLIONS)		AVERAGE ANNUAL RATE OF CHANGE 1930–60 (PER CENT)
		1930	1960	
"Service-Type" Occupations:				
Professional, technical, and kindred workers...	74.5	3.3	7.3	2.7
Managers, officials, and proprietors excluding farm....................................	69.0	3.6	5.9	1.4
Clerical and kindred workers.................	63.2	4.3	9.6	2.7
Sales workers...............................	84.3	3.1	4.8	1.5
Private household workers...................	100.0	2.0	1.8	−0.3
Service workers excluding private household..	91.8	2.8	5.8	2.5
Total..................................	76.0	19.1	35.2	2.1
"Goods-Type" Occupations:				
Craftsmen, foremen, and kindred workers.....	24.3	6.2	9.2	1.3
Operatives and kindred workers..............	19.9	7.7	12.8	1.7
Laborers excluding farm and mine............	27.4	5.3	3.5	−1.4
Farmers and farm managers..................	0.0	6.0	2.5	−2.9
Farm laborers and foremen..................	0.0	4.3	1.6	−3.5
Total..................................	19.2	29.5	29.6	0.0
Total, all occupations...................	50.4	48.6	64.8	1.0

SOURCE: 1930, U.S. Bureau of the Census, *Occupational Trends in the United States, 1900 to 1950*, Working Paper No. 5, 1958, Table 1; 1960, U.S. Bureau of the Census, 1960 Census of Population; Vol. I, *Characteristics of the Population*, Part 1, "U.S. Summary," Table 201, and "Occupation by Industry," Table 1.

Employment data are not available in this form, but gross product data in current and constant dollars are available and are reproduced in Table 4. There are important differences between services defined as expenditures and our definition of the service industries;[4] nevertheless, we find that the expenditure classification also shows a more rapid rate of centage accounted for by the service sector to rise.

Table 5 shows sector levels and shares for census years from 1870 to 1930. Services grew more rapidly than goods throughout the period; the average *differential* in rates of growth of employment was approximately 1.4 per cent per annum. Since 1929, the differential be-

[4] The expenditures method of classification treats government as a consumer rather than as a producer. Also, the value of the services of wholesale and retail trade and of many business service industries is assigned to goods rather than services.

TABLE 4

Gross Product by Type of Final Output in Current and Constant Dollars, 1929 and 1963

	1929 (Billions)	1963 (Billions)	Average Annual Rate of Change 1929–63 (Per Cent)
Current Dollar Output:			
Durable goods	$ 18.1	$110.4	5.5
Non-durable goods	38.1	179.8	4.7
Construction	11.2	65.2	5.3
"Goods" (including construction)	67.5	355.4	5.0
Services	37.0	228.4	5.5
Constant (1954) Dollar Output:			
Durable goods	30.8	96.3	3.4
Non-durable goods	64.7	161.8	2.7
Construction	26.1	53.0	2.1
"Goods" (including construction)	121.5	311.1	2.8
Services	$ 60.3	$181.4	3.3

Source: 1929, Office of Business Economics, *U.S. Income and Output*, 1958, Tables 1–6 and 1–7; 1963, *Survey of Current Business*, July, 1964, Table 65.

TABLE 5

Gainful Workers, Goods and Service Sectors, 1870–1930[a]

	1870	1880	1890	1900	1910	1920	1930
			Thousands of Workers				
Goods	10,330	13,875	18,370	21,780	26,360	29,870	30,770
Service	2,450	3,320	5,200	6,920	9,770	11,360	16,730
Goods excluding agriculture	3,840	5,170	8,200	10,860	14,770	18,470	20,020
Service excluding government and domestic service	1,410	2,100	3,490	4,880	7,080	8,740	13,350
			Per Cent of Total				
Goods	80.8	80.7	77.9	75.9	73.0	72.4	64.8
Service	19.2	19.3	22.1	24.1	27.0	27.6	35.2
Goods excluding agriculture	30.0	30.1	34.8	37.8	40.9	44.8	42.1
Service excluding government and domestic service	11.0	12.2	14.8	17.0	19.6	21.2	28.1

[a] Sector totals exclude a small number of workers in each year for whom no industry was reported. "Gainful workers" includes unpaid family workers and unemployed.

Source: U.S. Bureau of the Census, Sixteenth Census of the United States: 1940, *Comparative Occupation Statistics for the United States, 1870 to 1940* (Washington, D.C., 1943).

tween the two sectors has been slightly larger, 1.7 per cent per annum.

Until 1920, the shift to services could be explained entirely by the movement from agricultural to non-agricultural pursuits; employment in the goods sector, excluding agriculture, rose as rapidly as in services. After 1920, however, the rates of growth diverged; and, as we saw in the first section of this paper, in recent years employment in the non-agricultural goods sector has begun to decline absolutely as well as relatively.

REASONS FOR THE RELATIVE GROWTH
OF SERVICE EMPLOYMENT

Allan G. B. Fisher was one of the first economists in this century to emphasize the strength of the trends we are examining in this paper. His book, *The Clash of Progress and Security*, published in 1935, is perceptive and contains much that is relevant to the problems of 1965.[5]

Colin Clark's writings on this point are better known, particularly his often-quoted conclusion, "We may well now turn to examine what much careful generalization of available fact shows to be the most important concomitant of economic progress, namely, the movement of working population from agriculture to manufacture, and from manufacture to commerce and services."[6]

Neither Fisher nor Clark offered a systematic analysis of the factors responsible for the growth of services; both tended to stress sector differences in income elasticity and changes in productivity. Professors Kuznets and Stigler have questioned the existence of significant differences in income elasticity,[7] and a recent econometric analysis questions the alleged difference in productivity.[8] This section considers some evidence concerning both matters.

INCOME ELASTICITY OF DEMAND

When the income of a family or a nation rises, so does its demand for most goods and services.[9] The ratio of the percentage increase in demand to the percentage increase in income is referred to as the "income elasticity." When the percentage increase in demand is equal to the percentage increase in income, the income elasticity is unity. Individual items of consumption that have elasticities greater than unity are said to have elastic demand, while those with elasticities below unity are characterized as inelastic. The question at issue here is whether services, in the aggregate and at the individual industry level, face demands that are more elastic than the demand for goods.

A clear-cut answer to this question is difficult to obtain for a number of reasons. Some of the most important are:

1. To calculate elasticities, we need

---

[5] London: Macmillan & Co., 1935. E.g., "When we reach a level of wealth where the provision of personal services becomes economically important, the importance of the limitations of physical natural resources in the narrow sense steadily diminishes. We are then much more concerned with the exploitation of human capacity (which is also perfectly 'natural') and the maintenance of a moving equilibrium in a progressive economy comes to depend more and more upon the effective organization and education of human capacity" (p. 38).

[6] *The Conditions of Economic Progress* (1st ed., London: Macmillan & Co., 1940), p. 176.

[7] Cf. Simon Kuznets, "Quantitative Aspects of the Economic Growth of Nations, II, Industrial Distribution of National Product and Labor Force," *Economic Development and Cultural Change*, Supplement, July, 1957; and George J. Stigler, *Trends in Employment in the Service Industries* (Princeton, N.J.: Princeton University Press [for the National Bureau of Economic Research], 1956), p. 161.

[8] Phoebus Dhrymes, "A Comparison of Productivity Behavior in Manufacturing and Service Industries," *Review of Economics and Statistics*, XLV (February, 1963), 64–69.

[9] The exceptions are often referred to as "inferior" goods, e.g., potatoes.

measures of real output or consumption; but for many service (and some goods) industries, accurate measures of real output are not available.

2. Many industries produce intermediate outputs (sold to other firms) as well as final outputs (sold to consumers). Changes in income will affect intermediate demand as well as final demand in ways that depend upon the relative proportions of services and goods used in production.

3. Changes in relative prices, tastes, and technology also affect demand.

4. Substantial changes in income are often closely associated with changes in urbanization, making it difficult to determine whether the observed change in demand is related to income or urbanization.

5. The demand for some goods and services seems to depend upon the distribution of income as well as its average level: e.g., furs, domestic servants.

6. The adjustment of spending patterns to changes in income may require time; thus, the pattern observed at any given moment may depend upon past levels of income as well as present levels: e.g., state and local government expenditures.

7. Elasticities change; what is true at one moment in time may not be true at another.

Despite these difficulties, it is possible to form some judgment concerning relative elasticities for goods and services. Let us look first at the differential rate of change of sector real output between 1929 and 1963, a period when real income per capita was rising appreciably. Other things remaining equal, a more rapid rise in real output for the service sector compared with the goods sector would imply a more elastic demand for services.

Many questions arise concerning the accuracy of available data on real output; therefore two alternative measures are presented. The first takes the Office of Business Economics series GNP in constant (1954) dollars as the measure of real output. This measure has frequently been criticized on the grounds that the implicit price deflators exaggerate the rise in the price of services relative to goods. This bias is attributed in part to the fact that for government and certain other service industries prices are *assumed* to rise as rapidly as wages and no possibility of an increase in real output per man is admitted. If this criticism is valid, then measures of real output based on gross product in constant dollars would tend to overstate the growth of goods output relative to that of services.

The second measure of real output that I use is based on gross product in current dollars. This assumes that the prices of goods and services changed at the same rate.[10] This measure probably overstates the growth of real output in services relative to goods, since it seems to me unlikely that the price of goods did in fact rise by as much or more than the price of services. One cannot be certain of this, however, given the difficulty of obtaining true prices for services such as education and health, where quality improvement may have been very great.

Because the probable bias runs in one direction for one measure and in the other direction for the other, the two

[10] Because industry differences in rates of change of gross product in current dollars provide a good measure of relative changes in factor inputs, this second version implies that real output per unit of total factor input changed at approximately the same rate in both sectors (see Edward F. Denison, *The Sources of Economic Growth in the United States and the Alternatives before Us* [Supplementary Paper No. 13] [New York: Committee for Economic Development, 1962], pp. 218, 219).

measures of relative changes in output may be regarded as outer boundaries within which the true measure probably falls.

Table 6 shows the sector differentials in rates of change of real output under each assumption. The differential rate of change of employment is included for comparison. The most striking conclusion that can be drawn from this table is that differential rates of change of real output were very small relative to those for employment. This suggests that sector differences in income elasticity of demand were probably also small.

It can be seen that the results for the four comparisons are similar; the principal differences can be explained by the relatively slow growth of agriculture and rapid growth of government. The following discussion is based on the full-sector comparison shown in the first row. Under the first assumption (I) about output, demand for goods rose slightly faster than for services, but this might be the result of the change in relative price of goods and services rather than a difference in income elasticity. Under this assumption (gross product in constant dollars), the implicit sector deflators show that the price of goods declined relative to the price of services. The fact that service ouput rose almost as rapidly as goods output, over a period when the price effect alone would have caused a shift to goods, suggests that the income elasticity for services may have been slightly higher than for goods.

Under Assumption II (gross product in current dollars), real output in services rose 0.4 per cent per annum faster than in goods. This implies a slightly higher income elasticity for services because under this assumption prices rose at the same rate in both sectors, and there is no price effect to be considered. Thus both assumptions about real output point to the same conclusion concerning relative income elasticities.

Moving from the sector aggregate to the industry group level increases the uncertainties concerning the measurement of output and the possible effects of price changes, but the following rough qualitative judgments seem warranted. Income elasticity of demand for agriculture was probably appreciably below average. Output in this industry grew much more slowly than in other industries,

TABLE 6

SECTOR DIFFERENTIALS IN RATES OF GROWTH OF EMPLOYMENT AND REAL OUTPUT, 1929–63

(Per Cent per Annum)

Sector Differential[a]	Employment $(E_s - E_g)$	Output Assumption I[b] $(O_s - O_g)$	Output Assumption II[c] $(O_s - O_g)$
Service minus goods	1.7	−0.1	0.4
Service minus goods*	1.0	−0.3	0.1
Service* minus goods	1.4	−0.3	0.4
Service* minus goods*	0.7	−0.6	0.1

[a] For sector definitions, see note to Table 1. E and O = average annual rates of change of employment and output; s and g = service and goods sectors.

[b] Output measured by GNP in constant (1954) dollars.

[c] Output measured by GNP in current dollars.

Source: Output—1963, Office of Business Economics, "GNP by Major Industries, 1963," *Survey of Current Business*, September, 1964; 1929, based on Martin L. Marimont, "GNP by Major Industries," *Survey of Current Business*, October, 1962. Employment—same as Table 1.

and this cannot be attributed to adverse price movement. The elasticity for government services was probably appreciably above average, as evidenced by a rapid rise in output. For most of the other industry groups, there is no strong indication of an elasticity significantly different from unity. Trends in real output suggest that transportation may have been below average, while communications and public utilities and government enterprise may have faced a somewhat elastic demand. On balance, the behavior of the individual industry groups suggests that the elasticity for the service sector may have been slightly higher than for goods, principally because of a low elasticity for agriculture.

It would be preferable to apply the concept of income elasticity to individual consumer goods and services rather than to a heterogeneous collection of sector and industry group outputs, which include many that are intermediate rather than final. I have, therefore, attempted to compare the relative elasticities for goods and services by regressing changes in receipts or expenditures per capita on changes in income per capita across the forty-eight states. The periods chosen were 1939–58 for retail sales and sales of selected services, and 1942–57 for selected expenditures of state and local governments. Comprehensive data were available by state for those years.

The form of the regression equation was

$$\log Q = a + b \log Y + E,$$

where Q = expenditures or receipts per capita in terminal year divided by expenditures or receipts per capita in initial year, and Y = income per capita in terminal year divided by income per capita in initial year.

Because the regressions were run in double log form, the regression coefficient b may be regarded as a measure of the elasticity between income and expenditures. The latter are measured in current dollars and are used as a proxy for real consumption. Price does not enter into the equation because it is assumed that the *change* in price was the same in all states. If this was true, then the change in expenditures in current dollars gives exactly the same regression coefficient as would the change in real consumption. To the extent that prices rose faster in some states than in others, the bias is likely to be in the direction of a positive correlation between changes in price and changes in income. The regression coefficients may be slightly biased upward for this reason.

The equations were fitted in both weighted (1958 state populations) and unweighted form. The results were similar. I regard the weighted form as the more appropriate because the underlying process (except in the case of government expenditures) has nothing to do with states as such. These are merely statistical conveniences for grouping the behavior of individuals. Moreover, weighting reduces the chances that a random event or reporting error in a small state can significantly influence the coefficients.

The results of this preliminary inquiry into a very complex econometric problem are consistent with the conclusions based on sector trends in output. Income elasticities appear to be slightly higher for services than for goods, but the difference is not statistically significant. The estimated elasticity for total retail sales of goods is 1.00, for total personal services 1.15, and for total state and local government expenditures 1.10.[11]

Interpretation of the results is complicated by the fact that changes in income were very highly correlated with changes in urbanization ($r = .90$ weighted and .79 unweighted). The latter may have affected expenditures for some goods and services independently of changes in income; because the correlation between the two variables was so high, it is very difficult to distinguish one effect from the other. Each regression was also run in multiple variable form, with changes in both income per capita and per cent urban as the inde-

[11] The standard errors of the regression coefficient are .06, .08, and .13, respectively. If one reverses the form of the equation and regresses change in income on change in expenditure, the indicated elasticities are 1.18, 1.44, and 1.90, respectively. I am grateful to Milton Friedman for calling this to my attention.

pendent variables, but in most cases there was no additional explanation of the dependent variable after allowing for the loss of one more degree of freedom. In general, it may be said that part of what we here call income elasticity may reflect increased urbanization.

CHANGES IN PRODUCTIVITY

In Table 6 we saw that given the assumptions stated earlier, little or none of the shift of employment in services could be explained by differential rates of growth of output. It follows, therefore, as a matter of accounting, that most or all of it must be associated with differential rates of change of output per man. Table 7 shows these differentials under both assumptions about real output.

It should be noted that the simple arithmetical partition of changes in employment into changes in output and output per man has certain limitations. There are causal relations between changes in output and changes in output per man; they cannot, therefore, be treated as completely independent factors. Relative gains in output per man may result in changes in relative prices. This will affect output shares because the quantity demanded is not likely to be completely inelastic with respect to price. On the other hand, relative shifts in output can affect output per man through economies of scale and the stimulus to technological change. The large difference between the differentials for these two variables, however, suggests that additional information about possible interactions between them would not alter the major conclusions.

That output per man grew much faster in goods than in services is clear beyond doubt, and that this differential largely or entirely accounts for the differential change in employment is also clear. Perhaps the most interesting implication of Table 7 comes from the last column, which shows that there was a very substantial difference in sector rates of growth of output per man even when we use a measure of real output that assumes output per unit of total factor input to have grown at about the same rate in both sectors.[12] The large differential in output per man that remains under this assumption must be explained by factors other than "productivity" (defined as efficiency in the use of all resources).

TABLE 7

SECTOR DIFFERENTIALS IN RATES OF GROWTH OF EMPLOYMENT AND REAL OUTPUT PER MAN, 1929–63

(Per Cent per Annum)

Sector Differential	Employment $(E_s - E_g)$	Output per Man Assumption I $(A_s - A_g)$	Output per Man Assumption II $(A_s - A_g)$
Service minus goods...	1.7	−1.8	−1.3
Service minus goods*..	1.0	−1.3	−0.9
Service* minus goods..	1.4	−1.7	−1.0
Service* minus goods*.	0.7	−1.3	−0.6

Notes and source: Same as Table 6. A = average annual rate of change of real output per man.

These other factors include differential changes in hours per man, in the quality of labor, and in capital intensity. In 1929, workers in the service sector tended to work longer hours than those in the goods industries. By 1963 this difference had disappeared. Assuming that the extra hours made some contribution to output, this change must account for part of the differential trend in output per man.

There is considerable evidence that after 1929 the ratio of capital to labor and the average quality of labor rose faster in the goods sector than in the

[12] See p. 9.

service sector.[13] What we do not know is whether this was the result of sector differences in the pace and character of technological change or a response to changes in relative factor prices.

CHANGES IN RELATIVE FACTOR PRICES

Two major long-term changes in relative factor prices in the United States should be considered. One is the rise in the price of labor relative to the price of capital; the other is the rise in the price of unskilled labor relative to skilled labor. All industries would be expected to react to these changes by substituting the less expensive for the more expensive factor, but there is no guarantee that the ability to substitute (i.e., the elasticity of substitution) is the same in all industries. It may be that the goods industries found it easier to substitute capital for labor and skilled labor for unskilled labor. To the extent that this was true, the goods sector's share of total employment would tend to decline.

The question is further complicated by the fact that, even if the elasticities were the same in both sectors, and no technological change is assumed, there remains an a priori case for believing that changes in relative factor prices would alter employment shares. This is because the distribution of factors was not the same in the two sectors.

On average, it may be said that inputs of unskilled labor and physical capital were relatively more important in goods-producing industries and skilled labor was relatively more important in services. Of the three factors, the price of unskilled labor has probably risen the most, the price of physical capital the least. Given certain assumptions concerning the elasticities of substitution between factors in both sectors, it can be shown that the service sector's share of total employment would tend to rise as a result of the changes in relative factor prices and the uneven distribution of factors in the base period.[14]

Thus far I have considered only changes in relative factor prices that were experienced equally by both sectors. But what if factor prices did not change at the same rate in both sectors? What if the price of labor, and especially of unskilled labor, grew more rapidly in the goods sector than in the service sector? The result would probably be a greater substitution of physical capital and skilled labor in the former and, therefore, a shift of employment shares to the service sector.

Two important changes in the economy since 1929 suggest that this differential change in relative factor prices actually occurred. The first is the growth of unions in goods but not in service industries. Between 1929 and 1960, the degree of unionization in the goods sector rose from 11 per cent to 48 per cent. Change in the service sector was from 1 per cent to 7 per cent.[15]

The newly organized industrial unions in automobile production, steelmaking, coal mining, and so on worked to raise wages in those industries, and in particular tended to concentrate on raising wages for unskilled and semiskilled labor. The unorganized service industries did not face the same bargaining pattern.

A second development, working in the

[13] See Fuchs, *Productivity Trends*, pp. 23–30, 35, 36.

[14] It is assumed that the constant Allen partial elasticities of substitution are the same between each pair of factors and the same in both sectors. I am grateful to Richard Auster of the Massachusetts Institute of Technology for the mathematical proof of this theorem.

[15] Calculated from data in H. G. Lewis, *Unionism and Relative Wages in the United States* (Chicago: University of Chicago Press, 1963), p. 250.

same direction, was minimum-wage legislation. Large portions of the service sector (particularly retail trade and services) were exempt from this legislation (prior to 1961) and therefore did not experience the same statutory increases for the price of unskilled labor as did the goods industries. That the service sector has increased its share of unskilled employment more than its share of total employment is evident in data on demographic characteristics such as age, sex, color, and education.

WILL THE SHIFT TO SERVICES CONTINUE?

If we had firm answers to the many questions discussed in the preceding pages, we would be in a better position to forecast whether the shift of employment to services will continue. The analysis of the period since 1929 does not suggest any inevitable trend. Sector differences in income elasticity appear to have been relatively small and, if we exclude agriculture, possibly non-existent. The difference in trends in output per man has been substantial, but it is probably attributable only in part to technological change and in large part to differential changes in hours, quality of labor, and capital intensity—changes that can be explained by circumstances peculiar to the post-1929 period. Research on income elasticities of demand and elasticities of substitution of factors, as well as detailed studies of individual service industries, should help to provide a firmer base for predicting the future. My present estimate, which is only an informed guess, is that the shift will continue. I suspect that some of our "basic" manufacturing industries will begin to resemble agriculture—i.e., they will experience rapid gains in output per man while facing demand curves that are relatively inelastic with respect to both income and price. New additions to the labor force may be absorbed, in part, by employment in new manufacturing industries and in construction, but most of the growth will probably require increased employment in services, or result in unemployment.

IMPLICATIONS FOR THE ECONOMY

The shift from primary to secondary production has had profound consequences for every industrial nation; in most the adjustment process is still going on. Similarly, the shift to the service sector probably carries with it significant implications for our economy.

To be sure, such an attempt to look into the future is subject to important qualifications. A shift in the relative importance of different industries is only one of many changes that are occurring simultaneously in the economy, and these other changes may tend to offset the effects of interindustry shifts. Also, these shifts themselves may set in motion changes with implications different from those discussed here. Nevertheless, given the rapid growth of the service industries, it is useful to consider differences between them and the rest of the economy with respect to labor, industrial organization, the demand for capital goods, and cyclical fluctuations.

LABOR

Several important sector differences in labor force characteristics are summarized in Table 8. Probably the most significant difference is that many occupations in the service sector do not make special demands for physical strength. This means that women can compete on more nearly equal terms with men; we find women holding down almost one-half of all service jobs compared with only one-fifth of those in the goods sector. We also find proportionately more older workers in services despite the fact that the more rapidly growing sector would tend to have a younger work force.

An additional reason women and older workers are attracted to the service sector is that it provides greater opportunities for part-time employment. Sector differences in the role of part-timers and the changes between 1948 and 1963 are presented in greater detail in Table 9. We see that trade and services, in particular, have employed large numbers of part-timers and that the number has grown appreciably in the postwar period. If data were available on those working fewer than thirty-five hours per week *voluntarily*, the difference between the sectors would probably be even greater than that shown in Table 9.

The situation with respect to self-employment is complex. According to the 1960 Census of Population, the two sectors have approximately equal numbers of self-employed. Agriculture accounts for the lion's share (63 per cent) of the goods sector, while self-employment opportunities in services are widespread throughout the sector, with the exception of government and non-profit institutions. The Census of Population undoubtedly understates the number of self-employed in services relative to goods, because corporate employees are classified as wage and salary workers, regardless of the size of the corporation.

The officers of small, owner-managed corporations are, for analytical purposes, similar to partners or individual proprietors. About three-quarters of such corporations are in the service industries.

It has been widely believed that opportunities for self-employment are diminishing in the United States; but, if one excludes the decline of agriculture,

TABLE 8

LABOR FORCE CHARACTERISTICS, GOODS AND SERVICE SECTORS, 1960[a]

Row	PERCENTAGE OF U.S. TOTAL IN		AS PERCENTAGE OF SECTOR EMPLOYMENT	
	Goods	Service	Goods	Service
1. All employed[b]	50	50	100	100
2. Females	29	71	19	46
3. Over 65	41	59	4	5
4. Part-timers	41	59	19	27
5. Self-employed	50	50	13	13
6. Union members	85	15	48	7
7. More than 12 years of school	32	68	13	30
8. Fewer than 9 years of school	63	37	38	22

[a] For sector definitions, see nn. a and b to Table 1.
[b] Data in this table for civilian employment only; unpaid family workers are included.
Source: Rows 1–5, *U.S. Census of Population, 1960*; row 6, H. G. Lewis, *Unionism and Relative Wages in the United States*, Chicago, 1963, p. 251; rows 7–8, NBER tabulations of the 1960 *U.S. Census of Population* one-in-a-thousand sample.

TABLE 9

PERCENTAGE OF WAGE AND SALARY WORKERS WORKING FEWER THAN 35 HOURS BY INDUSTRY, 1948 AND 1963[a]

	May 1948	May 1963	Change, 1948–63
Goods (excluding agriculture)	9.6	10.6	+1.0
Service	16.3	23.8	+7.5
Mining, forestry, and fisheries	11.3	7.9	−3.4
Construction	16.2	16.9	+0.7
Manufacturing	9.1	9.4	+0.3
Transportation and public utilities	6.3	9.7	+3.4
Wholesale and retail trade	14.7	24.1	+9.4
Finance, insurance, and real estate	7.8	12.5	+4.7
Service industries	23.7	30.7	+7.0
Public administration	5.3	8.7	+3.4

[a] For sector definitions, see nn. a and b to Table 1.
Source: *Hours of Work*, Hearings before the Select Subcommittee on Labor, first session, on HR 355, HR 3102, and HR 3320, Washington, D.C., 1963, Part I, p. 78.

this is no longer true. In recent years, due largely to the growth of services, the self-employed have grown absolutely and have been a constant fraction of total nonagricultural employment.[16]

The role of self-employment in the future will be determined by several conflicting trends. A continued shift to service industry employment will tend to favor self-employment, but this may be offset by the influx of young workers and women into the labor force, since these groups are predominantly wage and salary workers. There may also be some tendency toward larger firms within each individual industry, but there is little reason to think that the door to self-employment will be closed as long as services continue to grow.

Given the importance of females, part-time employment, and self-employment in the service sector, it is not surprising to find a vast difference in the importance of unions in the two sectors. The service industries thus far have not responded very enthusiastically to organizing efforts, and the continued growth of this sector may mean a decline in union influence in the United States. On the other hand, if unions are successful in organizing the service sector to the same extent as the goods sector, we may see a significant change in the nature of the union movement.

The last two rows of Table 8 reveal interesting sector differences in education. The service industries make much greater use of workers with higher education and relatively less use of those with only limited schooling. This is not true for all service industries, of course, but it is true for the sector on average.[17]

There is another implication concerning labor which is not readily apparent in the statistics but which is potentially of considerable importance. For many decades we have been hearing that industrialization has alienated the worker from his work, that the individual has no contact with the final fruit of his labor, and that the transfer from a craft society to one of mass production has resulted in depersonalization and the loss of ancient skills and virtues.

Whatever validity such statements may have had in the past, a question arises whether they now accord with reality. The advent of a service economy may imply a reversal of these trends. Employees in many service industries are closely related to their work and often render a highly personalized service that offers ample scope for the development and exercise of personal skills.[18]

This is true of some goods-producing occupations as well, but there is little doubt that direct confrontation of consumer and worker occurs more frequently in services. To be sure, within many service industries there is some tendency for work to become less personalized (e.g., teaching machines in education, self-service counters in retailing, and laboratory tests in medicine); but with more and more people becoming engaged in service occupations, the net effect for the labor force as a whole may be in the direction of the *personalization* of work.

It should be stressed that the possibility of deriving satisfaction from a job well done and of taking pride in one's work are only possibilities—not certainties. Teachers can ignore their pupils;

---

[16] See John E. Bregger, "Self-Employment in the United States, 1948–62" (Special Labor Force Report No. 27), *Monthly Labor Review*, January, 1963.

[17] The higher *level* of education of service industry employees should not be confused with the fact that *changes* in the level of education have been greater in the goods sector.

[18] E.g., health, education, entertainment, personal services, repair services.

doctors can think more of their bank balances than of their patients. The salesman who must go through life with an artificial smile on his face while caring little for his customers and less for what he sells is often held in low regard. But at their best many service occupations are extremely rewarding and the line between "work" and "leisure" activity is often difficult to draw.

Some service occupations, notably those involving personal service, are not well regarded in this country. A study of why so many Americans consider personal services to be degrading would be very useful. It may be a cultural lag, rooted in the level of income and the distribution of income that prevailed in this country and abroad in the eighteenth and nineteenth centuries.

When the average level of per capita income in a country is low, the amount of personal services rendered is probably a function of the distribution of income. It is probably also related to social immobility and inequality of opportunity. In Europe, where there was more inequality and more immobility, there was probably proportionately a much greater consumption of personal services. These services were rendered by the low-born and the poor to the privileged classes and the wealthy. Americans probably tended to associate personal services with this inequality and noticed that there was much less of it in the more democratic United States.

It can be argued, however, that there is nothing inherently degrading in personal services. In a country with a high average level of income, one should expect that a large amount of personal service will be consumed and that a large number of people will find employment in that way. This would be true even if the income distribution were completely egalitarian. High per capita income implies high average output per man. This is likely to mean *very* high output per man in some industries (where capital can be substituted for labor, and technological change is rapid). Employment, therefore, will probably be primarily in those industries, such as personal services, where output per man advances slowly. Our attitudes toward personal services are not immutable laws of nature; they can be changed. Such a change would, I suspect, reduce unemployment and increase consumer satisfaction.

INDUSTRIAL ORGANIZATION

The shift of employment to the service sector carries with it important implications for industrial organization in the United States because the size of the "firm" and the nature of ownership and control are typically different in the two sectors.

In goods, with some notable exceptions, such as agriculture and construction, most of the output is accounted for by large profit-seeking corporations. Ownership is frequently separate from management, and significant market power held by a few firms in each industry is not uncommon.

In the service sector, on the other hand, and again with some exceptions, firms are typically small, usually owner-managed and often noncorporate. Furthermore, nonprofit operations both public and private account for one-third of the sector's employment.

Table 10 summarizes some of the available information concerning the distribution of employment in different service industries by size of employer. The size distribution in manufacturing is included for comparison. In wholesale trade, retail trade, and selected services, accounting for more than 50 per cent of the service sector, half of the employment is in companies with fewer than twenty workers. In finance, insurance, and real estate, 40 per cent is in very small firms. Another large fraction of service-sector employment is accounted for by self-employed professionals and domestic servants, not shown in the table. They represent the extreme in small size of employer.

Private (i.e., non-governmental) hospitals are considerably larger than the typical service firm; but even so, more than half the total employment of these institutions is in hospitals with fewer than 500 employees. Similarly, only relatively few private schools or colleges could be classified as large.

Government, which is often referred to as a "huge bureaucracy," actually includes many small employers. It is worth noting that employment at the local level of government now exceeds that of state and federal (civilian) government combined. One-half of this local employment is in governmental units with fewer than 500 employees.

One statistic that epitomizes some of the trends already discussed is the percentage of the national income originating in business corporations. Ever since the development of the private corporation, its role in the economy has tended to grow; but its relative importance apparently reached a peak about 1955, when corporations accounted for 55.8 per cent of total national income. Since then there has been a tendency for this fraction to decline, and in 1963 the level was 53.8 per cent, approximately the same as in 1948.[19]

[19] Data on national income originating in corporations and in the total economy are published by the National Income Division of the Office of Business Economics in the *Survey of Current Business* and associated publications.

Other things being equal, the shift to services tends to increase the relative importance of small firms in the economy. There are, however, forces within many industries that tend to increase the size of the average "firm." The pressure for consolidation of school districts and other local government units is a notable example. Bank mergers is another. The net effect of these countertendencies is difficult to predict.

TABLE 10

PERCENTAGE DISTRIBUTION OF EMPLOYMENT BY SIZE OF FIRM OR EMPLOYER IN MANUFACTURING AND SELECTED SERVICE INDUSTRIES

	EMPLOYMENT SIZE	
	Fewer than 20	Fewer than 500
1. Manufacturing (1958)	7	38
2. Wholesale trade (1958)	47	93
3. Retail trade (1958)	56	78
4. Selected services (1958)	57	87
5. Finance, insurance, and real estate (1956)	41	67
6. Hospitals (non-governmental, 1963)	n.a.	52
7. Local government (1962)	n.a.	49

Source: Rows 1–4, Bureau of the Census, *Enterprise Statistics: 1958 Part I, General Report*, p. 30, adjusted to include self-employed proprietors by assuming that they are in firms with fewer than twenty employees; row 5, Betty C. Churchill, "Size of Business Firms," *Survey of Current Business*, September, 1959, p. 19, adjusted for self-employed proprietors as rows 1–4; row 6, American Hospital Association, *Hospitals*, Guide Issue, 1964, estimated from distributions by number of beds; row 7, *Census of Government, Compendium of Government Employment*, 1962, estimated in part.

Industries in which small firms account for the bulk of the output typically do not present industrial control problems of the "trust-busting" variety. On the other hand, the growth of such industries may increase the need to guard against the restrictive practices of trade associations and professional organizations. Small firms may pose another problem for the economy because it is alleged that they do not allocate sufficient resources to research and other activities with large external benefits.

The growing importance of the non-profit sector will probably pose some disturbing questions about how to promote efficiency and equity in such organizations (cf. the problems with Blue Cross). When non-profit operations represent only a minor exception to an essentially private-enterprise economy, the problem is not very serious. But if we ever reach the stage where non-profit operations tend to dominate the economy, we probably will be faced with the need for radically new instruments of regulation and control.

DEMAND FOR PHYSICAL CAPITAL

There are some portions of the service sector that use large quantities of physical capital. Real estate and the services provided by government roads and highways are notable examples. By and large, however, goods industries tend to be more capital intensive than services. In recent years (1960 through 1963) business expenditures for new plant and equipment in goods industries were approximately three times as great as in profit-seeking service industries; the comparable ratio of output levels in the two groups of industries was only 1.25 to 1.00. Corporate plus non-corporate depreciation charges as a percentage of industry gross product reveal a two-to-one ratio in favor of the goods sector, and balance-sheet data from the *Statistics of Income* also suggest that capital intensity in the goods sector is roughly double that of the service sector.

There are, to be sure, exceptions to the general rule. The hotel and motel industry has a high capital-to-labor ratio, as do self-service laundries and dry-cleaning establishments, bowling alleys and motion-picture theatres. But in many important service industries, the input of physical capital is small. In barber and beauty shops, for example, labor and materials account for between 80 and 90 per cent of total cost. Another point to be noted is that in the largest service industry, retail trade, an important part of the capital input takes the form of inventories rather than the output of the capital goods industries.

In pointing out the relatively lower capital intensity of most service industries, I am not attempting to revive a "stagnation" theory in any form. The maintenance of high levels of employment and a rapid rate of growth is logically consistent with a decline in the relative importance of physical capital in the economy. The important point is to recognize that, if such a decline occurs because of interindustry shifts, it may be a proper and useful adjustment to new circumstances, with important implications for relative profit levels in different industries. While the national rate of savings may be just as high as before, other forms of investment, such as education, that are not customarily included in savings-investment estimates may take on increased importance.

BUSINESS CYCLES

It is generally believed that the service sector is less sensitive than the goods sector to cyclical fluctuations in production and employment. Daniel Creamer found that the cyclical amplitude of fluctuations of wage and salary payments of commodity-producing industries exceeded that of distributive industries, while the latter were more cyclically sensitive than wage and salary payments in the services.[20] The intersector differences

[20] *Personal Income during Business Cycles* (Princeton, N.J.: Princeton University Press [for the National Bureau of Economic Research], 1956), p. 47. Creamer's distributive group includes trade and transportation.

were greater during the cycles preceding World War II than in the postwar period, but the ranking of sectors in terms of amplitude of fluctuations was unchanged.[21]

In an unpublished NBER study, Geoffrey Moore has compared the fluctuation of employment in a group of nonagricultural commodity-producing industries with that of a group of service industries for four postwar business cycles (1945–61) and has found the amplitude to be much greater for commodities. The average monthly change during contractions was −0.75 per cent for goods and −0.04 per cent for services. The average monthly change during expansions was 0.35 per cent and 0.28 per cent, respectively.

Evidence of the greater stability of services can also be found in unemployment rates of wage and salary workers. Table 11 presents the average rate by sector and industry group annually for 1948–63 and the average for the sixteen years.

We see that unemployment in goods has been consistently higher than in the service sector; the average rates over the period were 5.8 and 3.8 per cent, respectively. Much of this differential can be explained by a greater amount of *seasonal* unemployment in goods-producing industries. The Bureau of Labor Statistics estimated that in 1957 the unemployment rates for seasonal reasons alone were as follows: agriculture, 2.7 per cent; construction, 4.2 per cent; manufacturing, 1.5 per cent; and transportation, 0.8 per cent; whereas in trade the rate was 0.6 per cent, and in services only 0.3 per cent.[22] Another possible explanation for the sector differences is that unemploy-

TABLE 11

UNEMPLOYMENT RATES OF WAGE AND SALARY WORKERS, BY SECTOR AND INDUSTRY GROUP 1948–63

	Average 1948–63	1948	1949	1950	1951	1952	1953	1954	1955	1956	1957	1958	1959	1960	1961	1962	1963
Goods	5.8	3.9	7.3	6.1	3.4	3.0	3.0	6.7	4.9	4.6	5.4	9.2	6.7	6.8	8.3	6.4	6.4
Service	3.8	3.4	4.6	4.6	2.9	2.4	2.3	3.8	3.4	3.0	3.4	4.9	4.3	4.3	5.1	4.4	4.5
Goods excluding agriculture	5.7	3.8	7.4	5.9	3.4	3.0	2.9	6.6	4.8	4.5	5.3	9.2	6.6	6.7	8.2	6.3	6.2
Service excluding public administration	4.3	3.7	5.1	5.1	3.2	2.8	2.6	4.4	3.9	3.5	3.8	5.5	4.9	4.8	5.9	5.2	5.1
Agriculture	7.0	4.7	6.5	8.2	3.9	3.9	4.7	8.0	6.4	6.5	6.7	9.9	8.7	8.0	9.3	7.3	8.9
Mining, Forestry and Fisheries	7.6	2.9	8.5	6.6	3.8	3.4	4.9	12.3	8.2	6.4	6.3	10.6	9.7	9.5	11.6	8.6	7.5
Construction	10.1	7.6	11.9	10.7	6.0	5.5	6.1	10.5	9.2	8.3	9.8	13.7	12.0	12.2	14.1	12.0	11.9
Manufacturing	5.3	3.5	7.2	5.6	3.3	2.8	2.5	6.1	4.2	4.2	5.0	9.2	6.0	6.2	7.7	5.8	5.7
Durable goods	5.3	3.4	7.4	5.2	2.6	2.4	2.0	6.5	4.0	4.0	4.9	10.5	6.1	6.3	8.4	5.7	5.4
Nondurable goods	5.3	3.6	6.9	6.0	4.0	3.3	3.1	5.7	4.4	4.4	5.3	7.6	5.9	6.0	6.7	5.9	6.0
Transportation and public utilities	3.7	3.0	5.2	4.1	1.9	1.9	1.8	4.8	3.5	2.4	3.1	5.6	4.2	4.3	5.1	3.9	3.9
Wholesale and retail trade	5.1	4.3	5.8	5.8	3.7	3.1	3.0	5.2	4.3	4.1	4.5	6.7	5.8	5.9	7.2	6.3	6.2
Finance, insurance, and real estate	2.1	1.6	1.8	2.0	1.3	1.5	1.6	2.0	2.1	1.4	1.8	2.9	2.6	2.4	3.3	3.1	2.7
Service industries	3.9	3.5	5.1	5.0	3.1	2.6	2.4	4.0	3.8	3.2	3.4	4.6	4.3	4.1	4.9	4.3	4.4
Public administration	2.1	2.0	2.9	2.8	1.6	1.1	1.2	2.0	1.8	1.6	2.0	3.0	2.3	2.6	2.7	2.2	2.5

SOURCE: *Manpower Report of the President*, 1964, Table A-11.
NOTE: Industry affiliation is determined by the last job held prior to unemployment.

---

[21] *Ibid.*, p. 56.

[22] U.S. Bureau of Labor Statistics, *The Extent and Nature of Frictional Unemployment* (Study Paper No. 6, Study of Employment Growth and Price Levels, Joint Economic Committee, Congress of the United States, November 19, 1959), p. 52. It should be noted in passing that the large sector differential in unemployment implies a subsidy of goods by services via unemployment compensation (see Charles B. Warden, Jr., "Unemployment Insurance, a Statistical Study of Massachusetts Experience" [unpublished Ph.D. dissertation, Harvard University, September, 1963], p. 82).

ment tends to be higher in declining or slow-growing industries than in those with rapid rates of growth of employment.

Of greater interest in the present context than the difference in level is the fact that unemployment in goods is much more sensitive to business conditions, as may be seen in Figure 3. The rate for each sector in each year has been plotted services is the fact that the output cannot be stored. This sector, therefore, is spared the effects of swings in inventory investment, swings which make a major contribution to the cyclical fluctuations of the economy. Similarly, some service industries do not experience cyclical changes in demand comparable to the fluctuations in consumer and producer demand for durable goods. Figure 4 shows

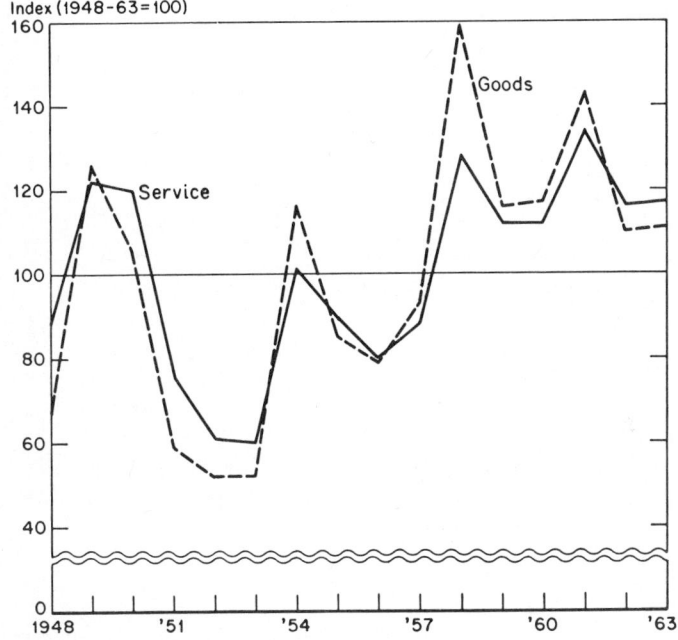

FIG. 3.—Annual indexes of unemployment rates, goods and service sectors, relative to their average rates, 1948–63. See Table 1 for sector definitions.
Source: *Manpower Report of the President*, 1964, Table A-11.

as an index number with the sector's average rate 1948–63 equal to 100. We note that the index for goods fluctuates much more sharply than for services over the business cycle. The variance of the goods index is more than a third larger than that of the service index.

The larger cyclical amplitude of unemployment in goods presumably reflects larger swings in output. One of the reasons for the stability of output in that cyclical swings of unemployment in nondurable goods manufacturing industries are less marked than in durable goods manufacturing. They are not as stable, however, as in services, even with government excluded. Greater cyclical instability in the purchases of goods than services is not inconsistent with goods having the same or even lower income elasticity of demand. The latter should refer to the relation between income and *consumption,* and the consumption of goods is much more stable than purchases over the cycle because of the existence of stocks in the hands of consumers.

It is difficult to obtain accurate data on cyclical swings in service industry output, as distinct from employment, but annual man-hours and real output (gross product in 1954 dollars) in wholesale and retail trade are shown as ratios of their 1947–63 trend values.[23] We see that the amplitude of fluctuation of real output is considerably greater than that of man-hours. The variance of the real-output

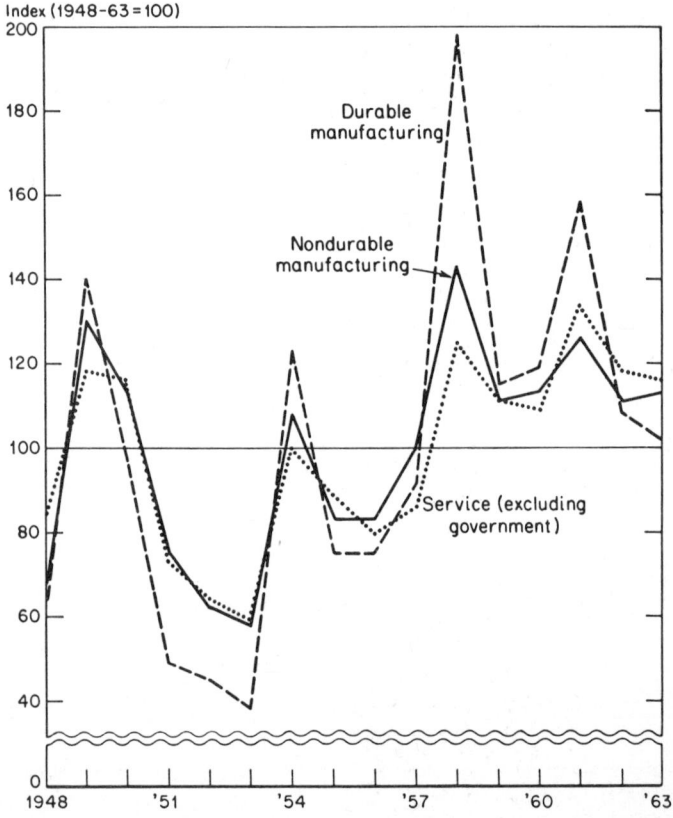

Fig. 4.—Annual indexes of unemployment rates, durable and non-durable manufacturing and service, excluding government, relative to their average rates, 1948–63.
Source: *Manpower Report of the President,* 1964, Table A-11.

in my judgment the amplitude of fluctuation in output is almost certainly greater than that of employment. Thus, inferences about stability, based on employment data, should be tempered in discussing output swings.

Some evidence to support this view is presented in Figure 5 (top portion) where series from the trend line is approximately double the corresponding variance of man-hours.

When a similar comparison is made for manufacturing (Fig. 5, bottom por-

[23] Trend values were calculated by fitting a least-squares regression line of the form $\log X = a + bT$, where X equals man-hours or real output, and T equals time.

tion), we find both man-hours and real output are more cyclically sensitive than in trade, but there is little difference between the variance of man-hours and of real output around their trend lines.

Reasons for the discrepancy between output and man-hours in trade (and other services) can be found in the nature of the labor force. First, there are large numbers of self-employed; their employment is almost completely insensitive to cyclical fluctuations in output. Second, the role of salaried employees, as opposed to hourly workers, is much larger in services than it is in goods. Also, the educational level is higher and the costs of hiring are probably greater. This means that dismissals or layoffs during recessions that are expected to be short-lived will be less frequent. Finally, it should be noted that there is a substantial number of service industry employees classified as "wage and salary workers" who are actually compensated on a "piecework" basis. Their wages in whole or in part are determined by their output, and take the form of commissions, tips, or a share of "profits." Employers

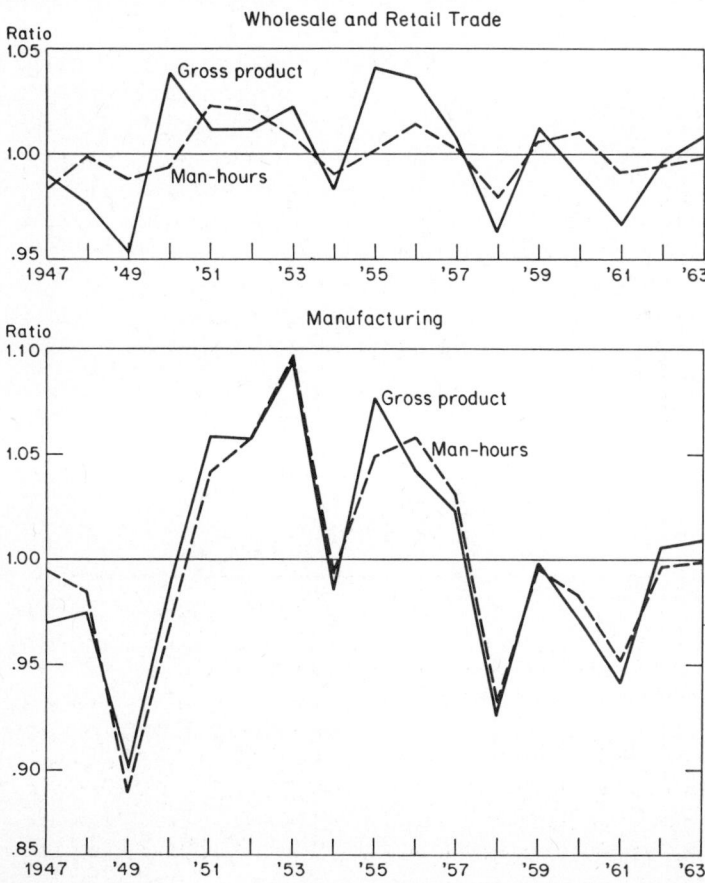

Fig. 5.—Ratios to trend, man-hours, and gross product in constant (1954) dollars, wholesale and retail trade and manufacturing, 1947–63.

Source: U.S. Department of Commerce, Office of Business Economics; U.S. Department of Labor; and *Economic Report of the President*.

have little reason to fire such employees when business falls off. This group includes real estate, insurance, and security brokers, waiters and waitresses, barbers and beauticians, and most salesmen of durable goods. Because their earnings are more sensitive to cyclical fluctuations in spending than are their hours of work, we can think of these workers as having "flexible" wages.[24]

There is some "piecework" employment in manufacturing, as well as in the service sector, but the effect on measured employment is not the same because of differences in the production process. When demand falls in manufacturing, the employer will probably cut back on production, regardless of whether labor is paid on an hourly or piecework basis, and this cutback will usually result in less employment. The effect in services is different because the amount and timing of the output and employment required is not known in advance. In both situations a decrease in demand means a fall in the marginal revenue product of labor. In manufacturing, the wage per hour tends to remain the same, and there is a reduction in man-hours. In the case of waiters, barbers, salesmen, and so on, employment tends to remain unchanged, and the necessary adjustment is achieved through a fall in hourly earnings.

A second interesting point suggested by Figure 5 concerns the timing of cyclical changes in real output and man-hours. Although annual data reveal timing differences imperfectly, in manufacturing the two series tend to move together, while in trade the man-hours series appears to lag behind real output. At most upper turning points, trend-adjusted man-hours reaches a peak one year after the peak in trend-adjusted real output.

[24] I am grateful to Jacob Mincer for this formulation.

The reason probably is that output in manufacturing can be planned in advance and the appropriate labor inputs scheduled accordingly. Output in trade is uncertain, and employment plans are often based on output experience of the previous year. It is relevant to note that the OBE measure of real output in trade does not make any allowance for such quality changes as delays in being waited on. It may be that when measured real output in trade rises rapidly, and man-hours do not, there is a decrease in the quality of service and therefore true output does not rise as rapidly as measured output.

To sum up, a comparison of the two sectors suggests that output in services is less sensitive to cyclical fluctuations in total demand and employment is less sensitive to fluctuations in output. Wage rates, on the other hand, are probably not as stable as in goods, because earnings frequently depend upon output. If the service sector continues to grow relative to the rest of the economy, these considerations will probably take on increased importance for questions of economic stability.

IMPLICATIONS FOR ECONOMIC ANALYSIS

In this section it is argued that the growth of the service sector has important implications for economic analysis. One line of reasoning is by analogy. In retrospect, it is apparent that the change in emphasis from primary to secondary production had considerable influence on economic analysis. Land became less important as an input in production and distribution models, and physical capital became much more important. The need for a theory of imperfect competition became more apparent. Short-run supply curves could no longer be thought of as completely inelastic, and the possibilities of increasing returns had to be examined with greater rigor.

One could argue that all the necessary theoretical tools can be found in one form or another in the writings of the earliest economists. The development and refinement of concepts, however, are often related to changes in the economy itself. Analytical work requires frequent compromises with reality. The compromises that may be appropriate, or the second-order effects that may be neglected, in an economy dominated by agriculture and manufacturing may turn out to be inappropriate, or too important to be neglected, in an economy dominated by the service industries. I shall try to illustrate this point by reference to the analysis of productivity and growth.

THE CONSUMER AS A FACTOR IN PRODUCTION

One lesson that our study of productivity in the service industries keeps forcing upon us is the importance of the consumer as a cooperating agent in the production process. To the best of my knowledge, this point is neglected in the analysis of productivity in goods-producing industries, as well it might be. After all, productivity in the automobile industry is not affected by whether the ultimate drivers are bright or stupid, or whether they drive carefully or carelessly.

In services, however, the consumer frequently plays an important role in production. Sometimes, as in the barber's chair, the role is essentially passive. In such cases the only conceptual adjustment called for is to recognize that the time of the consumer is also a scarce resource.[25] But in the supermarket and laundromat the consumer actually works, and in the doctor's office the quality of the medical history the patient gives may influence significantly the productivity of the doctor. Productivity in banking is affected by whether the clerk or the customer makes out the deposit slip—and whether it is made out correctly or not. This, in turn, is likely to be a function of the education of the customer, among other factors. Productivity in education, as every teacher knows, is determined largely by what the student contributes, and, to take an extreme case, the performance of a string quartet can be affected by the audience's response. Thus we see that productivity in many service industries is dependent in part on the knowledge, experience, and motivation of the consumer. Consider, for instance, what would happen to service-industry productivity in the United States if technology and capital and labor inputs remained as they are, but the consumers were exchanged for 190 million consumers chosen at random from India.

In a similar vein, productivity can be and often is affected by the level of honesty of the consumer. If consumers can be trusted to refrain from stealing merchandise, to report prices and costs properly at check-out counters, to honor verbal commitments for purchases and other contracts, for example, there can be tremendous savings in personnel on the part of producers of services.[26] These savings are probably important when comparisons are made with productivity in other countries or with the same country at different points in time. It may be that qualities such as honesty are themselves functions of the general level of productivity and income. A full analysis of productivity, therefore, requires consideration of these interrelations.

---

[25] See Gary S. Becker, *A Theory of the Allocation of Time* (IBM Research Paper RC 1149 [New York, 1964]).

[26] Changes in the honesty of employees have implications for productivity in the goods sector as well as services; changes in the honesty of consumers have implications primarily for services.

LABOR-EMBODIED TECHNOLOGICAL CHANGE

A second example of an analytical implication of the growth of service-industry employment concerns the labor embodiment of technological change. Labor embodiment is analogous to capital embodiment; it refers to a situation where the technological change or the advance in knowledge has its effects on productivity by being embodied in new additions to the labor force. For example, if newly trained doctors, after receiving the same amount of schooling as their predecessors, now know more about disease and are more effective in treating sick people, we should attribute the increase in output to labor-embodied technological change.

Most previous discussions of embodiment have concentrated on physical capital.[27] It has typically been assumed that capital is a fixed factor and that labor is variable, as in the following statement by Salter. "By investing in fixed capital equipment an entrepreneur gives 'hostages to fortune'; a decision to employ fixed capital equipment is irrevocable in contrast to labor, which can be discharged at will."[28] This may be a reasonably satisfactory description of the situation in manufacturing, but it will not do for much of the service sector. In fact, given the growing opportunity to rent capital equipment (e.g., computers), the reverse is sometimes closer to the truth. If one argues that rented capital equipment represents an irrevocable commitment for society, if not for the particular firm or industry using it, the same can be said for the supply of labor, and the distinction loses all force.

Let us imagine, for instance, a technological change in some government activity—a change that requires new skills on the part of labor. Civil service rules may prohibit the firing of old employees, and it may be difficult to train them in the new techniques. The full benefits of the advance, therefore, will not be realized immediately. If this type of technological change occurs at an even rate, the rate of change in productivity in government will be unaffected even though the level may be less than optimal.[29] But such changes probably do not occur at a smooth rate. If the output of the government agency is accelerating rapidly, it is likely that new additions of capital and labor are being made and that they can incorporate the latest technological change, thus raising the average level of productivity. This may be one reason that changes in output and changes in productivity are sometimes found to be positively correlated.

The argument applies not only to government but to all instances in which specific individuals are attached to specific organizations for long periods of time (through contract, moral commitment, or high hiring costs) and cannot easily be replaced by others. Such long-term attachments are common in many service industries. To be sure, the existing labor force may frequently be trained or adapted to take advantage of technological change, but in many cases this is not easy to accomplish. Economics professors who lack modern mathematical

---

[27] See W. E. G. Salter, *Productivity and Technical Change* (Cambridge, Mass.: 1960); R. M. Solow, "Technical Progress, Capital Formation, and Economic Growth," *American Economic Review Proceedings*, LII (May 1962), 76–86; and E. F. Denison, "The Unimportance of the Embodied Question," *American Economic Review*, LIV (March, 1964), 90–93. For reference to labor embodiment see Gary S. Becker, *Human Capital* (New York: NBER, 1964), p. 143.

[28] *Productivity* . . . , p. 38.

[29] Current methods of measuring output in government *assume* no change in productivity. This discussion is concerned with the effects on true productivity.

techniques provide a good example close to home.

The question may be raised why, if technological change is embodied in new entrants to the labor force, do we usually find that older workers earn more than do new entrants with the same number of years of schooling? The answer is, of course, that employers place a value on the experience and the maturity of the older worker which more than offsets the value of the labor-embodied technological change. If one could compare two workers of equal experience and maturity, one with the education of twenty years ago and the other with the current model, there is little doubt that the latter would command higher earnings. This is particularly evident in fields experiencing rapid technological change, such as engineering, where recent graduates often earn as much as old-timers do despite the maturity and experience of the latter.

The concept of labor embodiment is likely to be most relevant when formal schooling and job security are important, as in the professional and technical occupations. Three-fourths of all professional and technical workers are employed in the service sector.

CHANGES IN DEMAND AND PRODUCTIVITY

Another area where the growth of services may require some refinement of concepts is in the analysis of the relation between changes in demand and changes in productivity. In many service industries it is not enough to know by *how much* demand has changed in order to predict the effect on productivity. At least two other dimensions of demand in addition to quantity must be specified.

One source of variation arises because output is frequently uneven, with peaks coming at particular hours of the day, particular days of the week, and even particular weeks of the month. Such fluctuations are important for retailing, banking, barber and beauty shops, places of amusement, and some local government services. During non-peak times there is usually idle capacity. An increase in demand, if it occurs at these times, may result in very substantial gains in productivity. On the other hand, an increase in demand, if it occurs at times of peak demand, will probably not result in any increase in productivity.

A second source of variation is the "size of transaction."[30] This refers to the volume of business done with a single customer at a single purchase. My colleagues David Schwartzman and Jean Wilburn have found examples of service industries where increased demand, which takes the form of increases in the average size of transaction, results in greater increases in measured productivity than does an equivalent increase in demand that takes the form of more transactions.[31] George Benston has reported a similar finding for banking, and I suspect that this is true of many service industries.[32]

THE "REAL" GROSS NATIONAL PRODUCT

My final example of how the growth of services may affect economic analysis concerns the gross national product in constant dollars. This statistic is the key-

[30] Armen Alchian has a general theoretical discussion of this concept in "Costs and Output," in *The Allocation of Economic Resources, Essays in Honor of Bernard Francis Haley* (Stanford, Calif.: Stanford University Press, 1959), but he does not apply it specifically to the service industries. See also Jack Hirschleifer, "The Firm's Cost Function: A Successful Reconstruction," *Journal of Business*, July, 1962.

[31] There is some question whether the former should be called increased output or not. Under present conventions for measuring output in many service industries, it is recorded as such.

[32] "The Cost of Bank Operations" (unpublished Ph.D. dissertation, University of Chicago, 1964).

stone of many studies of productivity and economic growth. Unfortunately, it is probably becoming increasingly less useful for such purposes. The reason is very simple. Measures of real output in the service sector have always been unsatisfactory; as this sector becomes more important, the aggregate measure must become less satisfactory in the absence of significant improvements in the measures for individual industries.

Another trend working in the same direction is the decrease in market labor as a fraction of all time spent in productive activity. A small increase in the fraction of the adult population in the labor force has been more than offset by decreases in average hours per week and increases in vacations and holidays. Some of the increased free time may be spent in pure leisure, but probably the bulk of it is spent in the nonmarket production of goods and services and in consumer participation in the market production of services. As I have already suggested, how well or poorly these activities are carried out will surely influence economic well-being. Furthermore, both the output and inputs involved should be included in any comprehensive measure of productivity.

Economists have long been aware that the value of real GNP as a measure of output and economic well-being differs depending upon the level of economic development. There has been a presumption that the measure becomes more useful the more highly developed the economy.[33]

Up to a point it is probably true that the higher the real GNP is, the more reliable it is as a measure of economic welfare. But the trend may now be in the other direction, because at high levels of GNP per capita a large fraction of productive effort is devoted to services (where real output is very difficult to measure) and to other activities that are not measured at all.

An increase in home production at the expense of labor in the market reduces measured output because the former is mostly not included in the gross national product. If the outputs and inputs of home production were included, growth of this type of activity would probably tend to reduce measured productivity because of the absence of specialization and economies of scale. On the other hand, true economic welfare might be increased by such a shift if, as seems likely, labor in the market involves more disutility or less utility than labor in home production.

One example of the difficulty of measuring productivity and economic welfare at high levels of GNP per capita can be found in mortality statistics. At low or moderate levels of economic development, there is usually a negative correlation between real GNP per capita and death rates. However, now we have a situation where the United States GNP per capita is 50 per cent above the Swedish level, but life expectancy is considerably lower in the United States and the death rate for males 50–54 is double the Swedish rate. The reasons for this huge difference are not known, but are probably related to the pace of work, diet, exercise, as well as the output of the health industry.

I conclude that even as we increase our efforts to measure real output in the service sector, we must recognize that these efforts are likely to leave considerable margins of uncertainty. Future

---

[33] Simon Kuznets: "The importance of domestic activities relative to those that are part of the business system declines in the long run" (*National Income and Its Composition, 1919–1938* [New York: NBER, 1941]), p. 432.

studies of growth and productivity will probably find it necessary to develop auxiliary measures of "output" and economic welfare to be used in conjunction with the gross national product.

SUMMARY

The purpose of this paper is to report some tentative conclusions concerning the growth of the service industries and to indicate some implications of this growth for the economy and for economic analysis.

Between 1929 and 1963 employment in the service sector grew 1.7 per cent per annum faster than in the goods sector. At some point during the past decade the United States became the first "service economy" in the history of the world, that is, the first economy in which more than half of the employed population is not involved in the production of tangible goods. The more rapid growth of services was observed for individual industries as well as the sector aggregates and for occupations as well as industries. This shift represents an acceleration of a trend that has persisted for at least the past century.

Numerous conceptual and statistical problems in the measurement of real output make it difficult to explain precisely why service industry employment has grown so rapidly. The data examined in this paper appear to reject the hypothesis that the growth of real income per capita was a major explanation. The demand for services, compared with goods, may have been slightly more elastic with respect to income (principally because of the low elasticity for agriculture), but this was not an important reason for the shift of employment. Sector differences in the rate of growth of real output were probably very small; differences in the rate of growth of real output per man were probably very large.

The differential in the rate of growth of real output per man reflects a moderate differential change in productivity, in the sense of efficiency in the use of resources, but this is not the only or major explanation. It also reflects a more rapid decline in hours per man in services, a more rapid rise in the quality of labor in goods industries, and a more rapid rise in capital per worker in the goods sector.

The shift of employment to services has many important implications. The trends discussed here may be offset by other changes that are also taking place in the economy, but they serve to indicate the likely effects of the relative growth of services, other things remaining the same. These trends include:

1. Growing employment opportunities for women and older workers.
2. Growing opportunities for part-time employment and urban self-employment.
3. Growing need for workers with more formal education.
4. Possible decreasing importance of unions and growing importance of professional organizations.
5. Possible trend toward greater personalization of work.
6. Growing importance of small firms.
7. Growing importance of nonprofit organizations (public and private).
8. Declining relative importance of physical capital.
9. Growing stability in employment and, to a lesser extent, in output.
10. Possible increase in cyclical variability in output per man-hour.

In addition to having important implications for the economy, the growing relative importance of the services appears to have implications for economic analysis as well. One problem arises because the consumer frequently plays an important role in the production of services. This unmeasured input can have significant effects on productivity in retailing, health, education, and many other service industries. A second concept that may require further development is that of labor-embodied technological change. When, as in some services, formal education is important and there is job security, the rate at which advances in knowledge affect productivity will depend in part on how fast labor embodying these new advances can be added to the work force.

Another point concerns productivity and demand. The flow of production in many service industries is uneven, with sharp peaks at particular hours or on particular days, separated by periods of slow activity. Also, the size of the production run (the individual transaction) is often very small. For these reasons, the analysis of the relation between output and productivity in services will probably have to pay more attention to changes in the timing of demand and to changes in transaction size.

The final implication discussed is the likelihood that real gross national product is becoming increasingly less useful for studies of productivity and economic growth, because at high levels of GNP per capita a large fraction of productive effort is devoted to services (where real output is often very difficult to measure) and to other activities, such as "do-it-yourself," that are not measured at all. In the future, we shall probably find it necessary to develop auxiliary measures of "output" and economic welfare to be used in conjunction with the gross national product.